The Trees

Cheyenne Stevens

BookLeaf Publishing

India | USA | UK

Dedication

For my younger siblings
May your courage balance your caution and sate your curiosity.

For my darling, David
The poetry of my life and inspiration of my heart.

Preface

What was I meant to do? I asked this question in prayers for purpose thinking the answer would come in some form of productivity I could perform. I was hoping a talent, skill, or passion I have would create a way to help others and make money. But I've never heard this prayer answered in that way.

I was conflating purpose and meaning with its byproduct- responsibility. When I finally opened the Bible to search for an answer, I was pointed toward nature. Rocks, flowers, and trees are used as metaphors for obedience, patience and trust. I didn't see anything about the purpose of nature. I now believe the only explanation for the being of any living thing on Earth is that it pleases the Lord that it belongs there.

Freedom of belonging does include a freedom of expectations. All that are alive must pray, praise, and produce. We all must give more than we take from the Earth and each other. But this is a function of, rather than a purpose for, life. I've been contemplative-searching for ways to behave like that nature affectionately referred to throughout this collection as "the trees." This collection of poetry is the result of such questioning.

Please enjoy.

Acknowledgements

I would like to express my sincere gratitude to David K. Osbun and Kimberly I. Green for their guidance and care.

Protest Poet

Plump, pursed lips spill expletives
She's breakbeat, she slams
Her call cracks a megaphone
Into organized chants
And plastic pieces in
Blood-stained, cold black, streets were pounding
She's astounding
Now she's got something to say

She's got odes and sonnets
With cursive edges tucked into a bonnet
Her pen
Opens doors
Her pen
Is mightier than the sword
Her pen
Dancing over the lined paper
Making loops and sentences
Into loopholes in sentencing
Freeing imaginations of the prison ward
She's got the motherland in her vocal cords
Now she's got something to say

She's got the will of the free people

As a staff to guide the sheep
She knows everyone just wants someone
To tell them what to think
She sings the truth
Knowing what it can do
To the captive
Sings it to power
Hopes it catches on
Prays it catches on
Marching feet will carry her home
Did you hear?
Will you carry on?
Do you have something to say?

Civil

Mama worries, baby cries
Man in a nice suit lies
Brown man suffer, black man dies
Policing budget on the rise
Education budget compromised
Hungry people burglarize
Amazon workers try to unionize
Crypto is currency decentralized
(what?)
The metaverse ~~data farm~~ socialize
(what?)
Misinformation will polarize
The rent is getting too damn high
Can we get it subsidized
Deadly viruses: sterilize,
Wear your mask, sanitize
Foreign countries tyrannize
Military mobilize
Our boys at war and our allies
Fight! Fight! Organize!
The revolution will not be televised.

Taxes

Thinkin' we're so smart
The only ones
Can talk, read, and write.

Not knowing
We the only ones who need to.

The only ones can't
Read the memory of water
Pass it over and over
Our roots
Still and sure
Clothed, housed, and fed
Daily bread
All tax free.

The closest we got is
Making eyes at each other
On this couch

Some inside joke.

Vacation Days

I work overtime in the busy season
My tiny claws clutching the grating litter of the trees
Savory seeds and berries seasoned with earth.
I have fluffed and brushed my breast and tail,
But the naked fairies laugh
With their citrus perfume.
They are fire-mouthed, fancy children.
They say I use my pretty coat to cover
My bloating hips and belly.
I will stay behind.
Find peace when the dark time comes
And no one can work.
In winters quiet, roots will grow long
Because of my diligence.
The fairies will fly south
With the vapid butterflies.
They are sparkly nomads
Carried by warm winds
Invading foreign, fertile grounds.
They will whistle back
When I am slim
With my soft, preened coat
Smelling of new grass.
They will eat the flowering fruit of my labor

Wear an acorn hat
Rest in the oak shade.

To Do

I have so much stuff
Under the title to do
I got so many people
To answer to
It don't all fit
In 16 hours a day
So, I can't let sleep
Get in the way
Can't let the kids leave
Looking a-miss
Gotta have their clothes clean
And their hair done in twists
And the man need his work
Done on the hour
So, I'm skipping lunch and have
A coffee for power
Then I got to cook for
The one I adore
Then we've got chores
And chores and chores
And try to be fit or
In any good shape
Marching in place
Watching my plate

Church on Sunday, although
I haven't read my Bible
I haven't read at all
But my hands are never idle!
Trying to be a good woman
And carry the strain
Is goodness just production
Or is my living in vain?
Down on my raggedy
Knees I pray
Lord make it all go away!
Make those To-dos Ta-das today!

Lists

I must've made a million lists
Of things to do before I checked
Out,
But the housework is never done.

Some secret between the porcelain of the tub
And me,
As whisper I heard,
I poem I could read on the back of my eyelids,
The script of my veins,
 A date impending,
Versus and date impeding,
One more thing to do

Before I answer the aching
With the ever sweet nothing which answered the
question
"What do I do now?"
That kind of nothing never came
Nor did any other.
There is always something
To get done.

I always think

The trees don't have to live like this!
They don't go rushing about to nowhere
They just are nowhere.
They don't long for quiet
They just are quiet.
They never fall
Alone in the woods thinking
No one can hear me
No one can hear me
No one can hear me
No one can
No one and
So on and
So on.
They don't make lists to keep themselves alive
They just are alive.

I don't want to keep thinking about being
I just want to be.
Desk, pencil, and paper
Already present in my wood.
No need to cut it
Down. No need to plan
What's next. No need to answer
What now?
What in the world am I supposed to do now?

Windstorm I

I only whistle when
Begged by the wind
To dance together
To trace out shapes in the darkness
Casting shadows
Scratched through windows
And bent in time.

He remembers what I did.
He moves on.
Won't be back except to dance again.

Windstorm II

Winds whip and whistle
The house shakes
Darkness makes shapes
Phosphenes dance
As I open my eyes
To greet your
Slumber breaking.

You grab my waist
And pull me to a place
I am safe from the terrible howls.

Yor arms quiet the rushing.
I bury my head.
Our bodies build a shelter
From the powerful windstorm
Whistling through the night.
Warm under the blanket and
Safe from the sight.

Yellow Dandelion

Well, I stuck my yellow face up
Toward the heaven.
Bright and pretty me!
Bright and pretty me!
I let the cool breeze kiss my petals.
I let the raindrops soak my roots.
No one to water me or feed me
But the sky,
But didn't I know God would make a way?
Never in my life did I
See a set of steppingstones.
And I knew it was no garden,
For there was no husband,
But...

Maybe
I was a sunflower in a wild meadow.
'Til you made me feel common and raggedy, then
I was a dandelion in an unkempt lawn.

Blue Dandelion

We don't live in the neighborhood
They say we do
Just close enough that
They can charge extra:
Walking distance.
So, I walked to that neighborhood
And saw that everyone has flowers but us
So, I picked this bouquet:
Orange daylily from the bed of a winding driveway
Black-eyed susan from around somebody's tree
Periwinkle from a traffic circle
Ox-eyed daisy from a yard. I felt like it was calling to me
Russian sage from near a mailbox.
Brown-eyed susan intertwined with
Hedge bindweed from a bush
And blue dandelion from a road verge a little closer
To home

I know it's a weed
But I stuffed it in
Like I stuffed myself in this neighborhood
Me and the blue dandelion blending in
And me and the blue dandelion pretending
We're from the other side of this zip code

Me and the blue dandelion transcending our roots

My mother always said
We may be from the hood
But we're not of the hood
She robbed me of my native tongue
So, people where I come from
Ask me where I come from

But high class and hard classes don't mean
I don't belong here
Not that blue dandelion belongs anywhere
I picked a pretty pitcher
But there's pressure to
Pretend she's part of the group.
The other flowers whisper:
But isn't she from over there?
Well, she could've grown up anywhere
It was the gardeners who kept her away
 I didn't know the difference between her and Russian
sage
They're both the same shade
They both grow the same way
So, I put them both in this bouquet.

And now we have flowers, too

A Survey of the Cherries in my Mom's Yard

Some brown
Tired, slack into the ground
Some deep purple
Sitting on the lap of the roots, enjoying the shade
Some bright red
Tugging Mama's hand into the sun
Some greenies
At the teat

When the birds come, they don't complain
About screaming kids
And our hair in cherry stem knots
Playing superhero, preacher, and mother
They like the rhythm and tone of it

My mom would pick and wash
The deepest and sweetest
Before they went bad
And we'd eat 'til we were
Stained lips and fingertips
Us being high yellow
She'd pick and wash
Us too

So we were greased and shiny
For Sunday service

She will not be praised
For producing us alone
Like the cherry tree.

A Survey of the Cherries in my Dad's Yard

If there is no fruit,
Just pollen: the tree is male.
No judgement for him.

Tire Swing

I've never had a tire swing
Spinning, sailing, rubber, and rope.
A caged bird felt the same

Like her I've had my chance to sing
Thinning, wailing, sputtering hope
A nearly snuffed out flame

Heartbreak

When the white barren branches
Of December forewarned me,
I could hear their twigs
Scratch the wind.
They do not keep secrets.
They say what they know.

I came to visit in the spring.
They whispered pink and purple petals
Of infatuation into the wind.
Bright green sprouts grew in their place
Which I called substantial.

The evergreen shamed me
With her tsk.
She laughed that I called this substance.
Real green is spiny. Real green is strong.
But the sprouts became lush and thick, deep hunter.
Real enough for me.

Later I showed up to stay
With my passion red and fire orange
Packed up in my bags.
The trees were quiet,

Twisting away from me
Turned off
Just as they warned me.
They knew us all along.

Seedling

Everything wonderful within
That bone exterior
You wear to keep safe
From them birds
Keep safe beneath shoulders
Held high as your head
As your pride
Keep safe inside
Til you find time
To burrow

Taught boys can't
Cry their own water
Taught boys can't
Skip their own sunshine
Taught boys can't
Rest their own soil
Take the seventh year off

Taught men are machines to
Keep polished
    Not washed
Keep charged
    Not rested

Keep maintained
                    Not Fed
Be weathered but not weary
Conditioned as you may be
A seedling cannot grow into a machine

Burrow down in my breast
Humble mounds
Beneath my chin
I will cry you sweet water
You can lick from deep wells
In my collar bones
Tickling 'til I smile you a sun
And you stand up as someone new
Everything wonderful within
Now dangling from your nose
Earlobes and elbows

Scarcity seeks safety
Abundance provides safety
And now in the spring
Those birds
                    Have become a choir
That robot
                    Has become a man
That seedling
                    Has become a tree!

The Trees

I been thinkin'
The trees trust time
Cuz they are wiser
Than sadness

I been thinkin'
The green grass grows
Cut it don't know
about defeat

I been thinkin'
The fear is inside
Where butterflies
Make me unsettled

I been thinkin'
Of how to hush my mind
Til it's tree quiet
And how the truth could set me free

Breath

The trees breath in
What I breath out
We thank God for the air

What I breath in
The trees breathed out
Together we can share

I pose for sun
Salutations
The trees look up in prayer

The sun rise comes
The day's begun
The light is everywhere

Sunscreen

I let my cheeks and shoulders sunbake and bronze on an afternoon walk I took to round nearest to ten-thousandth step my tech wristwatch would clock for me.

I know it's misinformation that us blessed with vitamin D absorbing melanin can skip over SPF, but there's no denying; when you don't burn the sun feels good.

The sun feels like it wants to apologize for making you two-step shuffle with your clunky boots through winter's crunchy ice a while ago. The sun feels like it wants to tell you a fable and stare at you real close until you understand and then laugh with you. The sun feels like a mother telling you to take off your coat and stay a while. You at home just like the squirrels and the trees. You don't got to stand at the screen.

Couplet Affirmations

I am where I need to be.
Good things will happen for me.

I'm learning to keep standing still.
I'm learning I can trust His will.

I don't have to be afraid
When in His image, I am made.

He's working out good things for me.
I am where I need to be.

Sunday Ballad

Allow me to then shower you
With blown kisses from earth
The sound of music sent up too
Of praise, honor, and worth

A pretty dress and shiny shoes
A smile, a song, a tear
If I share joy and bear your fruits
Your presence will appear

Because I know the peace at hand
Because I know I'm free
Now pure, upright, and tall I stand
You've made me like a tree

The Secret of Stillness as Given to Me During Prayer

Anxiousness for the future
Will make you unholy,

When unsure of the future
Don't pray for revelation
Or provision- those are a given and guaranteed in His
timing.

Instead pray to be
Steadfast,
Unmovable,
Secure
Pray for your strength
Instead of praying out of fear

No need to fear the future
It is all in God's hands.

www.ingramcontent.com/pod-product-compliance
Lightning Source LLC
Chambersburg PA
CBHW071238140726
47996CB00007B/2656